The Written Collective presents...

I0080147

HEAR US ROAR

18 Simple Ways to Embody MORE Courage, Love, and Integrity

LENA ANANI | SALLY SCOFIELD | CRYSTAL SIMPELO

Disclaimer: The authors of this book do not dispense medical
advice or prescribe the use of any technique as a form of
treatment for physical or medical problems without the advice
of a physician, either directly or indirectly. The intent of the
authors is only to offer information of a general nature to help
you in your quest for emotional and spiritual well-being. In the
event you use any of the information in this book for yourself,
which is your constitutional right, the authors and publisher
assume no responsibility for your actions. *The named
characters depicted in this book are completely fictional.*

ISBN: 978-1-942104-16-2
LCCN: 2014919683

Printed in the United States of America

Collectively we will surrender to the wisdom of the Universe as it flows through us and manifests into the inspired words that will spill upon the thirsty pages on which we will write with our own gifted hands.

DEDICATION

This book is dedicated to YOU.

May you enjoy our words
with an open mind and a loving heart.

CONTENTS

ACKNOWLEDGEMENTS

We would like to thank the wonderful Amy Sue DeTar and the kind staff at the Sedona Rouge Hotel & Spa for their top-notch hospitality, delicious treats, and impeccable meeting spaces. Thank you from the bottom of our hearts for providing such an inspiring environment for us to write so freely in the magical place you provided for us. Your kindness and support will always be remembered!

HEAR US ROAR

It was a cold Chicago night in the dreary month of January 2014 when I had a heartwarming epiphany. Gently implanted in my mind's eye was this beautiful vision of cooperation and creativity in the form of the written word. Over the course of the next few days, I immediately took my vision and turned it into a live workshop unlike any other, and The Written Collective was born.

The Written Collective represents a time and space where like minded souls come together to connect and share in their own words a hand written message in unison to form a book for others to enjoy.

This book was written for YOU. What you'll experience in the following pages is the perfectly divine channeling of information written down in the moment as the Universe guided us to.

Not a single one of us takes any credit for any specific part of this book. Instead we share the credit for the whole book, as each one of us authentically infused our combined noteworthy wisdom into every chapter.

The Written Collective is the perfect example of what happens when creative souls come together to write without ego and without the need to be singled out as being better than any other author in this book. We simply decide to show up and step up to the challenge of writing one amazing, inspiring, and powerful book while being fully in the moment.

Hear Us Roar: 18 Simple Ways to Embody MORE Courage, Love, and Integrity was collectively written in less than 10 hours by Sally Scofield, Crystal Simpelo, and me (Lena Anani). We dedicated one magical weekend in the energy-infused town of Sedona, AZ to allow our words to flow seamlessly for the good of all, sharing one positive message after another.

All of us were completely in awe of the entire journey and the beautiful gifts it produced along the way, while recognizing that the words we expressed were not only meant for you to read, but were also clearly meant for us to digest as well… and we graciously did.

Enjoy this book. Return to it often. Read it cover to cover, or randomly flip to any of the pages for some on-the-spot divine guidance. No matter how you choose to use this book, we know you will resonate with these words just as much as we did.

Thank you for allowing us to share our thoughts with you, and we would love to hear from you, too. Contact us! Don't be shy!

May you always feel good and make magic…

Lena Anani
Founder & Leader – The Written Collective

FREEDOM

It's all about having a choice, to be able to do what you want to do, no restrictions. It's about the great feeling of flow, nature, running through your veins. It's easy and natural. We are born with it. When we are true to it, there is a calm essence that we embody. Staying connected to it is of great importance for your soul.

When freedom is missing from our lives we may see imbalances and cloudiness in judgment. You may have a sense of disconnect in many areas of your life such as in your relationships and your passions in life. There may be things holding you back that are causing fear and will only block the flow of energy to really do what you love to do. It is up to you to make that choice.

We can easily choose to make freedom an important part of our lives. It's a simple decision you can make right now to release the ties that bind you. We can start small by taking small risks like shouting words of excitement and gratitude towards the sky, or running outside barefoot. Yeah, we might look goofy or get judged by others, but they only judge us because they lack the element of freedom in their own lives. Make every day count as you challenge yourself to live more freely.

Freedom gives a sense of lightness, air, and energy, like there are no boundaries. Knowing that possibilities are endless enhances our courage to live the life that we want… on our own terms – with no apologies. Any door that you want is open to walk through. Freedom is our natural birthright, so there is a knowing that our choices will work out and that we don't need to over think how it's all going to play out, step by step.

When we have the courage to do what we love, and do this with our own true integrity we will then have the freedom that will allow us to have peace, joy, and happiness. All these values are in connection with one another and by having a positive outlook on these values they will grow into endless possibilities.

POWER

Power is such a strong word. Throughout my life I have felt feelings of empowerment and it has been one of the many values I cherish. I feel a sense of power when I do the things I love to do. What is something that makes you feel powerful? We all have this feeling deep within us.

Living life without a sense of power leaves us feeling small. Our greatness is muted. Our passion is watered down. Our ability to live in integrity with our soul's true calling is non-existent, and we feel powerless. We find ourselves stepping into the shadows, feeling weak and without the courage to be who we were truly meant to be. Our sparkle fades into a sadness that attracts all the wrong people and experiences into our lives. It leaves us feeling incomplete.

When applying more power in our lives, it's good to remember fairness, as well as responsibility. Perhaps, it is taking control of a situation. There is a balance that can be integrated in this process.

Power, when applied in the best possible way, can be motivational and inspirational, not only for the person expressing it, but for the others witnessing it. The good that can be dispersed from it can be contagious. You can express your power by motivating, inspiring and leading others.

When we apply the value of power into our lives we feel like we can achieve anything. We feel like we have set all the building blocks to have a sense of stability. We feel joy and love in everything we do. We feel like we can make more positive changes. Think about what the world could be if we all incorporate power into our lives.

Standing in our power is so important. We must commit to doing this on a daily basis. We must have the courage to be bold, to be ourselves, and to live in integrity with who we truly are, powerful beings creating peace on earth as we live more authentically each and every day. How will you express your power today? Tomorrow? Next month? Next year? Just thinking about it makes you feel powerful... as it should.

TENDERNESS

One value we often neglect to acknowledge or embrace is tenderness. We are so consumed with achieving greatness that we forget to honor the sweetness of life. Being tender and kind towards ourselves is one of the most important and most effective thing we can do to fuel our need to succeed at whatever we put our minds too. Tenderness is a trait that we are born with and unfortunately disconnect with as the years go by. At some point in our lives we discover the importance of experiencing tenderness towards others and ourselves.

When tenderness is not embraced towards others and ourselves, we express criticism and meanness, the not-so-nice thoughts that are not beneficial to anybody on the receiving end. Tenderness is actually natural to us, so we "hurt" ourselves when we don't express it.

We can apply the value of tenderness with the simple act of LOVE. Love can be shown in so many ways and whatever way we want to express love will allow our tenderness to show. We can show our tender love onto people we know, don't know, to animals, nature, and most importantly, to ourselves. In showing our love we will open ourselves up to have the power to succeed and accomplish anything we want to do.

What happens when we embrace tenderness in our lives is we start to experience softness in life. Miracles of one kind gesture after another become part of our story. We begin to see doors open to a world of kind and loving relationships. Our circle of friends becomes more positive and supportive. The energy of tenderness returns to us ten-fold making life a beautiful experience for us and everyone around us. And we ultimately play a role in paying it forward. We become co-creators of a tender and gentle Universe.

Tenderness has such a sense of peace about it. Remember, it really does come naturally, but in these times of ego and "macho-ness" you must have the courage to be true to yourself and share tenderness with yourself and others.

JOY

Joy comes naturally. Looking at things and giving gratitude, multiplies this feeling. We're naturally attracted to these things, the things that make us happy. It's easy and flows. It's the feeling that we are on top of a mountain with a most wondrous view or being silly with the best of our friends. It can be found in so many places – just waiting for us to notice! Seeing it in others can be contagious and sharing it is a most precious gift. Take notice of what big and little moments or things bring you joy and relish them, and you will see them multiply before your eyes.

When joy is subtracted from our lives we may notice things in our lives to be difficult. We may notice lack in motivation and drive. When we do not have joy, it will then block any sense of sharing positive feelings. We may feel alone in the world. These are all feelings that can and will be changed for the better with the simple mood of joy and happiness.

We can easily invite more joy into our lives by waking up each morning and listing at least 3 things we are grateful for. Gratitude is an instant joy maker and doing it first thing in the morning will perfectly set the pace for a more joyous day. Later in the day, turn your focus outwards to the environment around you, and challenge yourself to look for the little things in life that will inspire you to feel more joy. Pay it forward by doing something nice for others, and enjoy the joy that comes along with doing such a thing. We can call a friend and share happy stories with each other. We can open up to the Universe and allow ourselves to see other forms of joy in front of us. There are many ways to incorporate joy into our lives, but we must vow to do it… daily.

The result of this is such a wondrous snow-ball effect. Compound theory for sure! As well as multiplying more joy into your life, you infuse it into others. It's contagious! Just *thinking* about this process is a joy! This is our natural state of being, really. Being in this energy automatically makes us magnets to attracting not only more joy, but other wonderful things and experiences into our fields. Isn't it great to know it can be so easy and natural to do?

Incorporating joy into our lives also leads us to a sense of peace. Letting yourself go in being your true self will only attract more joy into your life. Be courageous in the ways you bring joy into your life. Show your true integrity and let your joy shine. Our joy as a whole can be life changing.

RESPONSIBILITY

We all have responsibilities in our lives. Some are easier to see than others – responsibilities to our families, bills, or work. One responsibility that we may tend to overlook is our responsibility to choose the way we live. Think about what you see yourself doing in the future. Don't think about anything else but your true passion. Set aside any factors of doubt or fear. This is our responsibility, to choose what will bring us to that goal. No one else can make that choice for us.

When we give away responsibility of running our own lives to others, we give away our power. When we rely on others to be responsible for us and for our own outcomes, we open ourselves up to feel like victims. Nobody likes a perpetual victim, not even you! Taking back responsibility and opening up to opportunities that come with it, will not only allow you to feel empowered, but you will begin to feel like the creator of your own life. Without responsibility, we are just lemmings following the lead of other people who don't really care about our well-being. When we don't take responsibility for our own actions and experiences, we leave ourselves feeling very vulnerable in a way that does not serve us.

What does responsibility look like to you? Rather than blaming somebody else for an undesired outcome, are you stepping up to the plate and considering your part in the equation? All of our actions have consequences, so try being conscious of the little and big things you do because they not only affect you; but others as well. Let's use responsibility in the most conscious way possible to make this a better world.

When we are responsible for our thoughts, actions, and lives we will see some awesome changes in our lives. These choices will then have a domino effect on everything else the Universe throws at us. We will feel like we will always have the power to choose our thoughts and actions. We will know that we can live our lives to the fullest and enjoy life more. Have the courage to just dive in and make the right decisions. Trust in yourself and know your responsibility.

A sense of peace calms your mind, when you realize how taking responsibility for your own life is how you take back your own creative power. You'll suddenly find more courage to pursue the dreams you've always had. And being responsible for your experience keeps you moving forward in life with integrity. Every decision you make will always be the right one, regardless of the outcome or external circumstances, because you took responsibility for your own life and turned it into something magical.

PLAY

For the love of all things fun, just play! We easily get so wrapped up in our big to-do lists that we forget to enjoy the beautiful playground we live in. Play is such an important piece of the fun puzzle of life. Play encourages us to be more creative, to feel youthful, and to spread the contagious joy and laughter that comes with being an adult-sized kid. Play is a form of expression that opens your heart and allows more fun in your life. It is a blessing that many of us take for granted, but we really must embrace playfulness so much more. Imagine what life would feel like if we spent more time playing, then planning or doing things because we are adults.

When we restrict our playful nature, we become too serious and our lives become grey. We begin to shrivel up inside and our soul begins to die. We focus on structure more strongly and don't realize that play is the balance, where our creativity flows from. Our lives, as a whole, lose out and we are not the best version of ourselves. Relationships can suffer, as well as health and well-being. So why not embrace your play today?

There are so many ways to incorporate play into our lives; we can first think of ourselves as kids. Think about the things you loved to do as a child. At this stage in life we didn't have the constant worries of our busy to-do lists and work. Now that you think of these wonderful memories in your youth, think about what you really enjoy to bring out your inner wild child. Whether that means to bust out the colorful finger-paints or swing on a swing set, just have fun. Everything will all play out!

When play becomes a part of our daily life, what used to be mundane now becomes pleasurable. It's a beautiful thing! We find ourselves feeling giddy about life and all our responsibilities. We begin to see them as blessings. We find ourselves looking for ways to make our daily chores more fun. We create games to play to encourage us to get more done. Play ends up being a component in our life that strangely makes us so much more productive. And being a playful person is just so inviting. Think of all playful energies around us: the singing birds, the laughing children, the goofball adults. Everyone is playing and getting more done, so let us do the same!

It's easy to get wrapped up in the busy "to-dos" in life. It's also easy to be worried about what everyone else is thinking about you. But I dare you… I dare you to have the courage to play, because ultimately that is what your soul wants. Stay in integrity and explore your playful side. This will bring about a peace of knowing you are being true to yourself.

INTENTION

Things start with intention. It's the beginning of the process of knowing what you want. It's the first phase of reaching a destination or goal. Setting intention is a powerful piece of the process to get the ball rolling. When we set an intention, only then can we move on from there. It's a solid foundation to a journey. It's a place where we can have a bird's eye view of what we desire coming into fruition. It is Step 1. When we are clear about an intention, we can then move on into birthing this desire.

In our daily lives it is so easy to lose focus of our intention. So many factors play into falling through with our intentions. We may at times second-guess our end goal and let negativity and judgments sway our decisions. What happens when these blocks come into play is that we don't get the things done that we once trusted our intuition in doing so. By not following through with our desires, we then make excuses to not getting things done. We doubt and set ourselves up for failure in achieving our set goals.

Setting an intention for everything can become an easy habit. Start with the morning. When you wake up, feel free to set the intention for how you would like your day to happen. What do you want to accomplish? How do you want to feel at the end of the day? Your intention could also be part of your prayer routine. You can create your intentions every time you start the car. You can set an alarm on your phone to remind you to set an intention. Always be willing to define your intention and release it to the Universe so it can unfold easy and effortlessly for the highest good for all.

The result after setting an intention is the satisfaction of knowing that you clearly put it out to the Universe. Now you know that it can happen. Taking inspired action after setting your intention is what the next step will be. You now have confidence that this "order" you sent out will be completed. Things can either come into your presence, making things fall into place or perhaps opportunities will just "happen" to come to you, all by just doing the simple task of setting your intention.

Setting our intentions allows us to feel peace within ourselves in knowing that we can do what we put into the Universe. With courage and dedication, getting to that set goal will all help in the steps to success. Not holding back will also help us stay true to our integrity. Be yourself and your intentions will shine.

DEPTH

Dive right in! Have no fear to what can come from something. Prepare yourself and know that we can do whatever our hearts tell us to do. The depth of our soul is where our purpose and happiness is. Our depth is what makes us original and different from everyone else. It is up to us to find out what that is. Try it and you will see your inner depth, deep inside your core. Let the water take you where it wants to.

When we lack depth in our lives, we lack authenticity. When we lack authenticity, we lack joy. Depth keeps it real. Are you a deep person or a shallow one? Without allowing yourself to show your true colors, you're just being superficial. Your most attractive feature is hidden deep in your core and is waiting to bust out. When we keep it hidden, it becomes uncomfortable for us both inside our heads and out in the world around us. Life starts to feel unbearable and the people we've attracted into our lives are superficial, needy, and unhappy. When we lack depth we feel hollow inside.

So the next time you have the opportunity to express yourself, go deep. Peeling away the layers, like an onion, people will either relate to you or be more compassionate. (If they respond negatively – they most likely are not *your* people). Start to allow yourself to feel more – more joy, more sadness (let it out!), more play, and more peace. The connection that you and others have with your soul will be deeper and more fulfilling. It's exciting to know the possibility of you having "more" depth in your experiences.

When we find our true depth and authenticity we may start to notice we are attracting all the right people. We notice that the timing is right. We see the signs to help us reach deeper into our soul. We are able to allow and trust our gut in knowing that everything will always work out. We learn more about ourselves and reveal more about our true personalities. We are an example to others to just dive right in! Do you want to make this plunge?

Do you have the courage to dive deep into the depths of your greatness? Of course you do, that's why you picked up this book. You already know that when you express yourself deeply you are more in integrity with who you really are. Your authentic nature seeps out naturally and your mind is more at peace. The chaos of your thoughts slow down, because when you go deep the message is always clearer. Go beyond the surface because there's always more than meets the eye.

DELIGHT

It's always delightful when you allow the wonder of excitement into your life. Delight is such a playful word that brings up feelings of joy, warmth, and smiles. Delight is a word that can describe happy contentment, in an almost surreal state of peaceful bliss. When experiences are delightful, they tend to be mellow in nature but very nourishing for the soul. How delightful it is to know that experiencing delight can be so delicious! Bringing the element of delight into your life can be as simple as enjoying a perfectly created cupcake, or sitting peacefully by a water fountain, or just closing your eyes and replaying your favorite memories, all of which will bring out a smile.

It only makes sense that when we don't have delight in our lives; we bring in feelings of contrast. Rage, anger, resentment, and taking things for granted all fall on the opposite end of the scale of emotions. Feeling bad is not high on anybody's list of emotions, so notice when you are not allowing delight in. Feeling like the whole world is against you could resonate with you. It's a dark place that we can get swallowed into, if we do not take notice and let delight in. The light in our soul can be dowsed.

Some things we can do to bring delight into our lives are to do things you love to do. If we can't do it right this moment then the act of thinking of yourself doing this act works fine too. Do you like to dance? Then bring delight into your life by dancing to your favorite song. Meditate or go out into nature to open up your mind to be in a delightful state. Think about yourself shining bright, even in darkness. Surround yourself with delightful people. Feel happiness and joy in everything that you see, do, and feel in life. It will be delightful.

To state the obvious, creating new ways to incorporate more delight into your life will have you feeling simply delightful. You'll notice that your hunger for joy and wonder is satisfied with a little more room to continue your search for more delight. You'll notice yourself smiling more. The people around you are in good moods. You'll feel more playful and willing to explore life with wide-eyed bewilderment. You'll wake up every morning bright-eyed and bushy tailed. You'll start to notice all of the little things in life and grin from ear to ear. You may even start to wonder how you attracted such delight into your life. And you will be delighted to know that you deserve all the good you've attracted.

With what appears to be a sea of negative people out there these days, and the negative "media train", it takes courage to "stand out" and express delight. Delight, is such a soft, peaceful word, in a time where the "squeaky wheel" of rage and aggression gets all of the attention. Stay in your integrity and express your delight with the world! I promise you it's contagious.

SUPPORT

Support is a crucial part of life. To have a helping hand is all we need sometimes to get through. Whether it's someone we're actually leaning on physically or another ear we can confide in, it's important to know that we do not have to experience our journeys on our own. Sometimes just knowing that you have someone that will have your back is comforting and can give us the courage to do the things we dream to do. Sometimes it's the hardest thing to ask for… and when *that* thought comes up, it's most assuredly the thing we need most. So reach out. Reach out to your trusted network and ask for support. Most likely, your network will deliver ways you've never dreamed of to support you.

When we don't have a support system to help us and confide in we may start to feel down on our luck. We may feel like we are alone in the dark and can't find our way back. We may feel like there is no point to living. There may be feelings of sadness, fear, and depression. We may feel we are not worthy. We feel defeated, and that will only cause us to be down on ourselves even more. Have the courage to ask for help, and gain that support we need in life.

The easiest way to invite more support in our lives is to ask for it, simple as that. Reach out to a friend, a coach, or a mentor, someone you know in your heart could be the person that helps you get past the obstacle you're facing right now. Asking is always the hardest part, but when you get past it, all you get after that is support, lots of support. It's definitely easier to offer support than to receive it, but the reward is so much greater when you surrender to those who want to help you succeed. If you're worried about attracting the wrong kind of support or advice, then meditate and visualize yourself receiving the exact kind of support you need to be successful. Say a prayer and ask for the right kind of guidance when you need it most. We can always start there. Ask the Universe for support, and you will receive it.

When we choose to ask for and accept support, the doors will open up. They can open up in ways we've never imagined. Opportunities may arise from it. We may end up being able to do more than we could've imagined! Realizing this can be beneficial – perhaps now we can help more people on more levels. We can become bigger and better individuals that are more powerful. Our confidence may soar. We may have a strong foundation from which to build from. We can do anything! The possibilities are endless. Knowing that we don't have to do it alone can help bring us such comfort and ease in the process.

When we find that support in our lives, we have a sense of peace in our minds, knowing that we have people we can go to help us get through it. We have that courage to be in our own integrity and put ourselves out there, not being afraid of what can happen and just going with the flow. It takes courage to start a race, but step-by-step you will get there, with positive support, to reach the finish line, your set goal in anything you do.

COMPASSION

Compassion is love and love is compassion. Compassion is a feeling that we should all have for someone or something. Our lives and what we love to do are done with compassion. We all show compassion for our families, friends, and interests. It is that feeling within our hearts that makes us feel warm and tingly inside. It is that feeling we get when we just know it is right and everything will be just fine. We feel high vibrations when we are compassionate. We feel complete, with compassion in our lives. When we show compassion to ourselves we are able to show true compassion to everything around us.

When we don't apply compassion in our lives we open ourselves up to a bitter experience. We don't have positive, healthy, and nurturing relationships. Instead we invite feelings of anger, resentment, and fear towards others and ourselves. We open up to a world of one bad experience after another, not realizing how showing compassion toward others and ourselves is the key to change our perception of reality for the better. We become mean and cranky and blame the world for everything that goes wrong in our lives. We tend to judge others more and begin expressing it in a way that hurts everyone involved. Without practicing compassion, we are just plain old bullies.

Compassion towards ourselves may show up as nurturing, such as getting a massage. But it also can show up as loving thoughts, instead of negative mind-chatter. Compassion towards others may be holding a door for a person. This also may show up as having sympathy for what someone else has been through. A lot of times we judge people and their circumstances or the way they act. We have to remember to have compassion – we don't know what they have experienced in their lives to lead them to make the decisions they make or say what they say.

It's easy to overanalyze conversations and situations, but have compassion and know everybody's doing the best they can with what they have and what they know.

When we have compassion in our lives we will start to notice love in ourselves and in what we attract. We will start to see compassion come into our lives through our relationships and interests. Certain situations come up when we may least expect it, such as receiving a gift from someone or a random stranger complimenting you. We start to feel the love for ourselves more and more every day. We will then see ourselves spreading love onto others to form a ripple effect on the rest of the world surrounding us. Our vibration in this state of compassion can help the world in so many ways.

It seriously takes courage to be a person that shows compassion towards others. To open yourself up and be vulnerable is always a risk, but most of the time you end up with a peaceful outcome. It's also easier to be a person with integrity when you're being compassionate towards yourself and others; you are more in alignment with what you set out to accomplish in this life. Honor yourself and others in all areas of your life, and you will ultimately experience a happy sense of inner-peace.

BIRTH

When was the last time you birthed one of your most prized creative ideas? Some projects seem like they can be so time consuming that it almost feels like giving birth to a baby. These are the most rewarding experiences in life, not because of how enduring or exhausting it may seem but rather because of how powerful the result can be for you and for others as well. For example, birthing your first book after working on it for nine months, you look back on every step you took to help "your baby" grow into something that will change your life forever. Birthing the ideas you have within you is an amazing process that you will love and always appreciate for the rest of your life.

If we neglect to embrace the birthing process we can suppress our soul. We may be hard on ourselves and not think that we are worthy of birthing something. However, it's actually quite selfish to hide what we have inside and not share our gifts with others. The thought of the birthing process may seem painful, but it actually takes more of a toll on us if we don't. It may show up as depression or confusion about one's gifts. The most common misconception is that it won't be "good enough" or perfect, which can lead us to "creative paralysis".

There are things you can do to help this "birthing" process. Much like pregnancy, there are lots of changes that happen in our bodies that are physical, emotional, and mental. We get through these challenges slowly but surely, as long as we have the right mindset and intentions. What is it that you have always wanted to do, but have made excuses for not doing? Set that intention to doing it and imagine yourself feeling that end goal already in your mind. Let go of fear and worry and let everything take its course, because in the end we already know that everything is always working out for us to get there. Set small goals to get to that final end product. Trust in yourself and that all your decisions will only get you to that end result, and your "beautiful baby" will be born.

When we finally accept the soul's calling to birth an idea or project, we open the doors to world of new possibilities. We find ourselves surrounded by a new set of friends, or community, which expresses our soul's desire to express itself. We attract more positive conversations that inspire us. We feel motivated to continue birthing that which rewards us internally and externally. We may even get teary eyed more, because the joy we feel from birthing our purpose can be so profound. The joy we feel can be so overwhelming in a good way. Tears of joy will flow as you connect with this new inspired version of yourself. Laughter and grinning ear to ear is also inevitable.

No doubt that birth requires courage. But the peace that comes from taking that leap and being in integrity with your soul is one of utmost importance. It's a natural flow of life, and when we surrender to it, can be the most rewarding process. To nurture something as it grows makes you feel so glad, so proud, and fulfilled. To know that you could do it and you DID DO IT, a beautiful miracle in deed.

SURRENDER

Sometimes in life we feel the need to control. Surrender is more of the opposite. Let go. Let it be. Let it happen. Relax. Allow. Knowing that surrender is such an easy thing to do – it is not always our first reaction. We are in such a world of "making" things happen or manipulating for an outcome. Surrender is natural. It may come across as weak, but it may take a conscious brain, one that's been brain washed into constant action, to realize that surrendering is the best "action" to take. Turn it over to the Universe. All is well. Everything happens in divine timing. Surrender is bliss.

When we choose not to surrender to the Universe, we may start to notice that things are not working as planned. This may be because we are too focused on making things happen in san inauthentic way. We may start to feel scatter-brained at tasks at hand. We second-guess decisions and sometimes feel frustrated that things didn't go as planned. We can feel defeated. We can feel weak. We may then feel disconnected from our true authentic self at times. Stop, take a breath, and let it be. Things will be just fine.

There are so many areas in our lives that we neglect the opportunity to surrender. When we are rushing to get to a destination and find ourselves stuck in a traffic jam, we can simply choose to surrender to this situation and accept that we will arrive at the perfect time. When we set out to complete a project and the materials or timing don't seem to be working in our favor, we can surrender to the idea that maybe something better will happen. When we feel the need to control every day-to-day situation, task, or activity, we can reframe our thinking with a snap of our fingers to remind ourselves to surrender and let go. There may be a better plan for us than the one we are trying to make happen.

When we choose to accept this state of surrender automatically, we relax. Think about it. Think about a current example in your life and how you might want to surrender to it. Feel it in your body. All tension seems to wash away. In a sense, we are able to receive the good things that are trying to come to us on a normal basis that we have a wall/barrier up against. We feel a sense of peace and ease as support rushes in to our aid. More things can happen now.

There is courage in ourselves when we choose to surrender and let things be. When we allow for surrender we are at peace inside. This is when our true integrity is shown. Courage, peace, and integrity are all traits that can be shown through our surrendering of our worries to the Universe. It allows more room for the awesome experiences to happen. Surrender and trust in the Universe!

EXPECTANCY

Expectancy is the knowing of what you want. It is what you expect of yourself and others. Expectancy is how you expect certain situations to play out. When we have judgment about things, good or bad, we see things and envision things in certain ways. What we see and put out into the Universe is what is brought into our lives, like a reflection in the mirror and we have some expectation of ourselves, and hopefully what we see is love. What do you see and expect from yourself?

When we don't allow ourselves to have certain expectations, we dilute our power to manifest what we want from life. Some expectations we put in place can be harmful for us and for our relationships, so we've learned to let go of having any and all expectations. But we end up missing out on the magic of life. We don't allow ourselves to expect miracles, or to expect positive experiences, or to expect raises or rewards. We can certainly place our affirmations with expectation to witness the results we want, so long as we don't place expectations on others.

So the next time you know what you want/make an intention, expect that it will happen or something better! Having that trust is crucial for it to be brought about. Know that it is your divine right to have what you expect. That is what the Universe wants from you! Act as if what you are expecting is coming to you; or even better – if you can act as if you already have it. Embrace it; embody it. If you expect to have that new car, feel as if you are driving it. If you expect to have that fabulous body – feel it as you walk!

When we apply this expectancy in our lives, we will feel that magic. If we set that loving light and intention in our lives, we will receive. We will notice more and more things happen, even more than what we may have expected. We notice things will happen automatically in our favor at times. We may feel that we can do anything that our heart and mind asks for. We are more abundant in love, joy, and happiness. We see ourselves in loving, low maintenance relationships. We feel the magic in our lives; that is our right.

In order to live your life with integrity, you must maintain a certain level of expectancy. You know what you will and won't stand for, so to be in alignment with your beliefs, you'll need to have the courage to make decisions based on what you expect to experience. Expectancy, when used in a positive way, can also help you create more peace in your life. So take some time today to let the Universe know what you expect from it, and be ready to experience your magic.

DISCERNMENT

Discernment is being able to analyze the options in front of you. Often we act impulsively when we come to a fork in the road of our lives, and end up facing obstacles we didn't intend on experiencing. All paths lead to the same destination, but the path we choose could be easy and fun, or difficult and lousy. Using discernment helps us slow down our thinking and allows us to tap into our own powerful intuition to guide us on which direction to go in. Being discerning gives us a chance to weigh the pros and cons for a better outcome and experience with everything we pursue.

When we don't discern, we can get swept up into the latest fad. We may end up following what everybody else is doing for the sake of ease or the fear of being different. Not honoring your own discernment is not being true to yourself, your own intelligence and intuition. We are all being guided (whether we want to admit it or not; or trust in it or not) and we have the ability to tap into our own discernment at any time. When we don't discern, we are not choosing or deciding what is in our *own* best interest and we rob ourselves of our own authenticity.

When we discern in our lives and make a decision, know that by doing this it will lead you to that same destination. Even if we make a wrong choice, at least we have the realization that this route did not work for us. That is the positive. Positive thinking will help us through this. If we have problems making and choosing a path, relax and meditate on that choice. Put yourself in a good place. Take a walk, ride your bike, or listen to some music. Pay attention to the things around you and you will find an answer. Just know that anything you choose will have a positive outcome.

When we become more discerning, we tend to create a mellow yet magical life experience. We'll have fewer ups and downs. We'll be moving through life on the perfect plateau of good experiences. We make better choices. We have better relationships. We bring in a steady yet desirable income. We manifest what we want easily. We complain less. We feel more gratitude. We eventually learn to discern naturally, and it becomes our second nature. We learn to make better decisions, and we learn to actually make decisions instead of going back and forth. Most importantly, we become constant partners with our own intuition.

Discerning takes guts. Being able to decide on things using your own judgment, with your own "tools", relying on all of *you* is such a rewarding soulful experience. Knowing you can discern with confidence will bring about serenity in your decisions and ultimately build more and more of a trust with yourself as a whole. Remember… you've got this!

SPONTANEITY

Spontaneity is FUN! Flying by the seat of your pants is like a surprise gift that's waiting for you around every corner! It's energy; it takes action. It's always an adventure. Sometimes intuition can be categorized this way as you are learning to get in touch with yours. Spontaneity is a fresh view of doing things, unexpectedly. Spontaneity can come in the form of inspired action. You never know where it may lead, but can end up being most rewarding. It is pure excitement in a box that you get to choose. Feel the energy in that?!

When we don't have spontaneity in our lives we may fall in a place of repetition. We fall in a place that is comfortable and safe in our lives.

We are not having fun and start to fall deeper into a hole of darkness. We lose track of our passions in life. We miss out on great experiences. We stop the process of learning new things. We fear what change brings into our lives, causing us to live every day "safe".

We can be more spontaneous simply by doing something silly or goofy each day. You might look like a goofball to other people, but who cares? You're not responsible for their reactions or thoughts, only yours. So do something each day that will make your inner-child giggle with glee. You can add more spontaneity to your life by taking a different route to work each day, switching up your morning routine, or calling a friend randomly for no special reason other than just to say "hey". You can use spontaneity to perform random acts of kindness for other people. You can send out hand written cards of love and gratitude to your friends and family. You can start singing your favorite song in public, because it makes you happy. You can do whatever you want because you are spontaneous.

When we incorporate spontaneity in our lives the result is living a life with more freedom – the freedom to choose at a moment's notice. We hold more visible energy in our bodies, and it spreads into everything we do. Fun opportunities that we embrace lead to doors that open up, and abundance flows in. We radiate joy more, because we are excited about what life may bring us. Everything becomes an opportunity. It's like looking at the bright side of everything. The possibilities become more and more abundant. BIG surprises are activated in the most positive manner. Things we never thought would happen, actually happen!

Build up that courage to try new spontaneous things! This will show your true integrity. You will be surprised at what may happen, and hiding your true integrity is something we don't want to happen. We must be free with our souls and we will live lives of peace and happiness. Just jump right in and do something you've never done.

SIMPLICITY

Simplicity is plain and simple. It's the only thing we need to live our lives. It is as simple as paying attention to our thoughts. It's as simple as loving everything that surrounds us. It's as simple as having fun. It's as simple as smiling. It's as simple as "if you want to do, then do". It is simplicity in your thoughts and actions. Why make things complicated in life? Just simply let it be, and good things will follow. Simple as that, as long as we are aware of the way we perceive ourselves and the world around us.

When we don't approach life with simplicity, we make it more complicated. Usually it's because we are trying so hard to control the outcome of a situation. When we try to control things, we feel the need to map out every single step, and the experience ultimately feels rigid and uncomfortable. Simplicity allows for more flexibility so we can embrace a better outcome with less effort on our part. To make things complicated or intricate or confusing, we exhaust ourselves in the journey of following through with what we set out to do. Road trips and vacations become complicated. Projects become over-whelming. Relationships become high- maintenance. Work becomes daunting. Simplicity opens those things up to be a more pleasant experience.

So think now – what's important in your life? It's not what everybody else thinks. This automatically "weeds" out all of the clutter that surrounds you, whether it's your thoughts on a situation or simply your bedroom closet. Think, without over-analyzing, "Why do I want this?" When you feel your "drama-mind" come alive and try and complicate things, remember to "bring it back" and remember what's important to you. Nature for example, is as simple as it gets. This can be used as a guide for when things get hectic in your life. Even getting out in nature has a grounding effect to bring your mind a sense of peace and make it easier to see the big, simpler, picture.

When we accept simplicity into our lives we will notice that things don't have to be complicated. We will notice a focus in our lives that will make decision-making easier. We will start attracting other simple-minded people who also accept simplicity into their own lives. We start to see simplicity all around our world, which in turn will cause others to see through your example. We have clear vision of the big picture.

It's funny how we interpret the word "simple-minded" as something negative that means a person who is dumb or stupid. Perhaps it's time to redefine that word to mean a person who has the ability to create a simple and rewarding life. Because really, that's all we really want. Life in itself is already complicated; why do we feel the need to make it worse? Having the courage to label yourself as simple minded, and choosing a more simple way of life, is guaranteed to create a peaceful experience. Both your mind and environment will be at peace, and you will move forward easily with integrity in all that you choose to do with your magical life.

CELEBRATION

Most of us are great at celebrating special occasions like birthdays, holidays, and anniversaries. However, many of us forget to celebrate the smaller things in life. Celebration is the honoring of someone or something that makes your heart sing. Celebration is when your inner cheerleader steps out to support and recognize others on their special day. Imagine how empowered you'll feel when your inner cheerleader steps out to celebrate all of your small, yet impactful, accomplishments on a daily basis. Celebrating yourself is one of the best ways to keep you motivated to do great things. Celebrate as much as possible, because you truly deserve it.

If we choose to neglect to celebrate, we tend to take things for granted. This may squander our opportunities for more celebration or things to be grateful for. Things get boring and dull. A life does not seem worth living if there is nothing to celebrate – this may lead to depression. If we do not celebrate our accomplishments we may not realize our own potential and not think we are good enough. Celebration is a good way to keep us aware of what we are capable of.

We can all celebrate by doing many things. Celebrate your accomplishments every day. It can come down the smallest of things. Have you had such a great day? Celebrate it! Have you got a chance to see a friend after three weeks? Celebrate it! Have you had a chance to have some needed alone time to meditate? Celebrate that too! Celebration is a fun act that we can think about to make us feel good. Go back to a special exciting moment in your life and just imagine yourself in that same situation. Think and celebrate this moment and how you felt. Look at pictures of some happy experiences. These help us celebrate all the wonderful times we have had!

When we learn to celebrate more, we invite more reasons to celebrate. It multiplies, because by celebrating the good things in your life, you are telling the Universe that you want more of it. The Universe answers and continues to send you more of what you've been focusing on, and luckily for you, it's been all the good stuff you've been celebrating. Celebrate all the small things today, and you'll have plenty to celebrate tomorrow. Guaranteed!

Say "yes" to celebration! Have the courage to celebrate in what ways you want to, whether it's a big bash or rewarding yourself with your favorite bowl of ice cream. Feel the serenity that comes with knowing that you can do what you want to do, and that at the finish line, there's a sweet package of fulfillment to have fun and reward yourself for your gifts! In what way will you decide to have a finale of fireworks for you – because you totally ROCK!

ABOUT THE AUTHORS

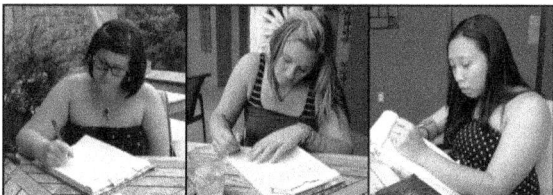

Left to Right: Lena Anani, Sally Scofield, Crystal Simpelo

*To watch a super fun and silly video
that we made to celebrate the
completion of our book, please visit:*

www.NoteworthyWisdom.com/HearUsRoar

Lena Anani is the passionate founder and creative alchemist of NoteworthyWisdom.com, a global community driven to experience life beyond the ordinary fulfilling their life's magical purpose.

She joyfully contributes to her community as an Author, Teacher, Intuitive, and Mentor. She combines over a decade of experience from both her corporate path and a healing path, using her left-brain project management experience in con-junction with her right-brain creative healer experience.

During her first few years of teaching, Lena was inspired to write her first book *Stop Look Listen: A Practical Guide to Intuitive Healing*, later wrote her second book *OMG Do It Now: Be the Voice You Want to Hear in the World*, and very recently wrote and published all in one day *Ignite Your Magical Purpose: How To Feel Good, Make Magic, And Create A Rewarding Life*.

As the Content Strategy Magician, Lena also coaches and mentors her clients by helping them design a successful authentic platform to motivate others as they share their noteworthy wisdom with the world.

She has helped several inspired authors write, publish, and promote their first book, and continues to help many more authors devise a successful plan to launch their book via BrainstormYourBook.com, her extremely popular and affordable coaching program for aspiring authors.

Lena's mission in her current lifetime is to enlighten and empower as many people as possible to create a ripple effect of unconditional love, and ultimately world peace.

You are invited to connect with Lena Anani anytime you want by emailing her at info@NoteworthyWisdom.com with your questions, your comments, or just to say hi!

Learn more about Lena Anani at:
www.NoteworthyWisdom.com

Sally Scofield is naturally drawn to serving others in a uniquely helpful way. She has taken on the other side of the meaning "lightworker" since moving on from being a lineman at a large electric company in Upstate New York.

Now she lights up a room with her presence and energy, emitting positive vibes wherever she goes. She is passionate about sharing her favorite manifesting techniques as part of the workshops she teaches locally.

Sally proudly and recently authored her first book *Light Up Your Soul: 10 Powerful Ways to Create a More Fulfilling Life* and is currently working on her next highly anticipated book.

She also loves to help people uncover their life's purpose through the proven, scientific based system of Hand Analysis.

Sally happily resides in her beautiful, peaceful home in Delhi, NY, with her significant other, Mike and their dog, Bud.

She is an avid nature woman, spending as much time outdoors as possible. She loves working with Icelandic Horses when she is not raising the consciousness of others or saving the world by lighting up one soul at a time.

Learn more about Sally Scofield at:
www.SallyScofield.com

Crystal Simpelo is truly an artist at heart. From the day she was born, she was obsessed with coloring which eventually evolved into her love of learning new ways to use that art.

As a kid, she also knew that she wanted to be a teacher. Now she currently facilitates "Heart to Art" workshops in the Chicagoland area, teaching people both art and meditation techniques, as she reminds her students the importance of the connection between heart and art.

Crystal took what she learned from teaching and recently authored her first book *The Colorful Expression of Your Soul: A Mandala Coloring Book & Meditiatve Creative Journal* and the ideas for the next creative project continue to flow.

Her professional expertise as an artist was established when she obtained her Bachelor's Degree in Fine Arts from the Northern Illinois University with a concentration on Interactive Art.

Crystal's creative nature is also extended into her Massage Therapy practice, where clients have raved about her as "THE best massage therapist and overall healer in the Chicagoland area."

She currently lives in her hometown of Lombard, IL with her loving husband. When she's not creating art from the heart, you can find her playing the piano, checking out live music, and hanging out with her friends.

Crystal's mission in life is to raise the vibration of this world and promote a positive state of being through art. Learn more about the author of *The Colorful Expression of Your Soul: A Mandala Coloring Book & Meditiatve Creative Journal* at CrystalSimpelo.com.

Learn more about Crystal Simpelo at:
www.CrystalSimpelo.com

NOTES

NOTES

NOTES